CARIBBEAN PIRATES
with Famous Pirate Rum Drinks

Arnold K. Elovaara

Contents

Art Design and Research by Arnold K. Elovaara
© Copyright 2005. Arnold K. Elovaara. All Rights Reserved.

Published and Printed by:

Scenic Art©

1-800-283-8765

Printed in China • PE.6.1005.000

PIRATE STRONGHOLDS
in the Caribbean

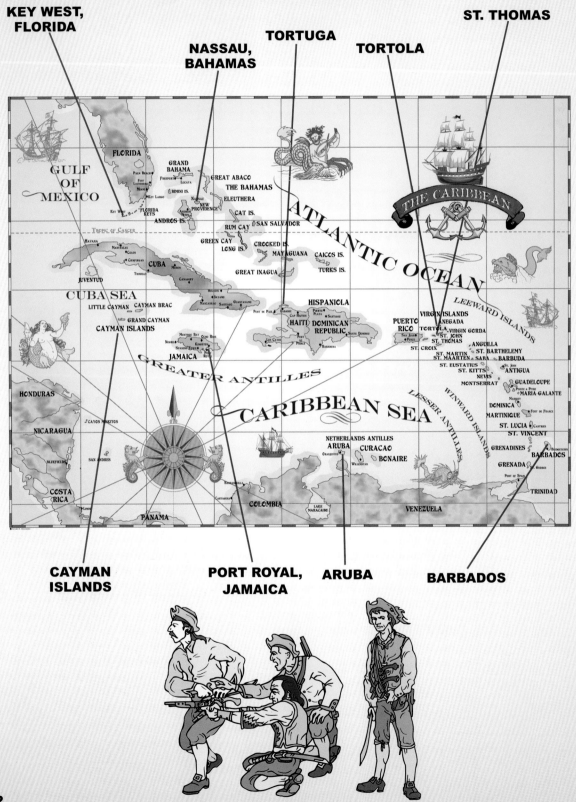

KEY WEST, FLORIDA

NASSAU, BAHAMAS

TORTUGA

TORTOLA

ST. THOMAS

CAYMAN ISLANDS

PORT ROYAL, JAMAICA

ARUBA

BARBADOS

CARIBBEAN PIRACY

**THERE WERE MANY POPULAR HANGOUTS
FOR PIRATES AND THEIR ACTIVITIES OF PLUNDERING
PASSING SHIPS IN THE CARIB BEAN. AMONG THE
FAVORITE "WATERING HOLES" FOR PIRATES WERE THE
PORTS OF NASSAU, TORTUGA, PORT ROYAL AND ST. THOMAS.**

Piracy in the Caribbean probably began in the 1600's and flourished in the decade following 1714. Since recorded history is somewhat vague as to the exact chronology of events about the pirates in the Caribbean, one has to rely upon the translations of historical writers in Denmark, France, Spain and Portugal. The English were fairly good at keeping Royal records which divulged the complicity of the English Crown in granting "Privateering Licenses" to an odd mixture of local pirates. These licenses permitted the pirates to attack and rob mainly the Spanish ships en route to Spain from Central and South America with their cargos of treasure and other valuable goods.

The pirate ships were commissioned with "Letters of Marque", making them auxiliaries of their Royal Navy. In return for the "purchase" of these licenses, the pirates agreed to share a good percentage of their spoils with the Crown of England. England at that time hated Spain. They were jealous of the fact that Spanish Royalty dominated many of the prime sources of New World gold and silver and important trade routes, many originating in the Far East where valuable cargos of silk, spices, china and other goods originated. Frequently, the Far East galleons loaded with goods, would land on the Pacific coast of Panama. Using local mules, they would transport the goods across land to other waiting galleons anchored near the Caribbean shoreline. From here the heavily laden West Indies galleons would then set sail to Europe via routes which often took them through the various Caribbean islands. Pirate ships based out of ports such as Nassau, Tortuga, Port Royal (Jamaica), Charlotte Amalie in St. Thomas, St. John, St. Croix, Tortola, and even Puerto Rico, would then attack and plunder the galleon's cargos.

CARIBBEAN PIRACY

AN OLD ENGRAVING OF THE HARBOR AT CHARLOTTE AMALIE, ST. THOMAS.
A VIEW OF THE FORT IS IN THE BACKGROUND

PIRATE SHIPS OF ALL SIZES AND SHAPES WERE USED TO ATTACK
PASSING TREASURE LADEN GALLEONS BOUND FOR EUROPE.

PIRATES AND BUCCANEERS

The word Pirate simply means "one that plunders and robs on the high seas". In some areas of the Caribbean, pirates were called Buccaneers.

The Buccaneers were originally an unorganized group of cattle and pig hunters that lived on the island of Hispaniola (now Haiti and the Dominican Republic). The word Buccaneer comes from the French word **boucan** which means barbecue. Ancient Arawak Indians living on Hispaniola are credited in teaching the newcomers the art of outdoor barbecuing the meat of animals, as well as preservation techniques which turned the meat into a form of jerky. The dried jerky was used to trade with passing ships for items such as tobacco, rum, salt, sugar, tea, flour, medicine, rum, powder and lead for the muskets. Eventually most Buccaneers living in the rolling hills of Hispaniola became tired of hunting and then reverted to piracy on the high seas.. often using proceeds from the group sales of dried meat to purchase a vessel for their plundering purposes. Directly off of north Hispaniola was an important trade route for the Spanish Main treasure ships. The nearby island of Tortuga served as a base of operations for the Buccaneers. Tortuga, having steep and high hills, allowed the Buccaneers to hire "vessel spotters" that sat in trees observing the ocean below. Once a potential ship was spotted, word spread fast down the hill to the crew of Buccaneers sitting at anchor. Then the Buccaneers would set sail and attack the passing ship.. usually one which flew the flag of Spain's King or Queen.

ARAWAK INDIANS BARBECUING FISH

A BUCCANEER LIVING ON HISPANIOLA WITH HIS HUNTING DOGS

AN EARLY BUCCANEER'S THATCHED HUT.
BUCCANEERS IN MANY WAYS, WERE RESPONSIBLE FOR STARTING
THE CARIBBEAN PIRACY MOVEMENT **WHICH LASTED FOR AT LEAST ONE HUNDRED YEARS.**

PIRATE SHIPS

PIRATE SHIPS GATHERED TOGETHER AT SOPERS HOLE, TORTOLA

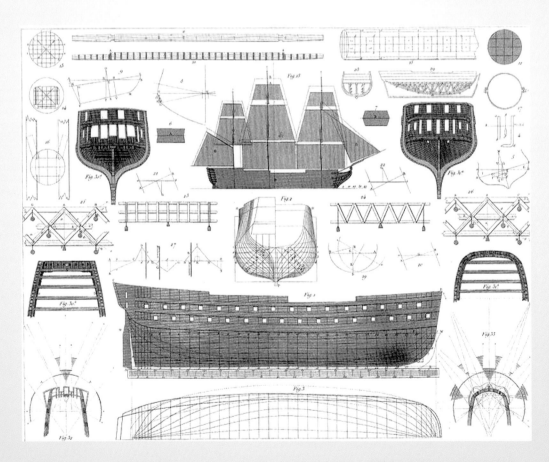

ACTUAL RARE CONSTRUCTION PLANS FOR A TREASURE GALLEON

PIRATE SHIPS

1680-1724

Pirates ships came in many different shapes and sizes. Pirates often preferred small sloop style boats that were able to attain high speeds and quiet operation.. especially for night attacks. One great advantage was that the small sloops were able to retreat to shallow coves for protection from ships that required deeper water.

PIRATE SLOOP, NASSAU

PIRATE SLOOP, VIRGIN ISLANDS

PIRATE SLOOP, PORT ROYAL

OFFSHORE PIRATE SLOOP

TWIN-MASTED PIRATE SHIP

ENGLISH NEF

38 GUN SPANISH GALLEON

SPANISH TREASURE GALLEON

LIFE ONBOARD

The crew on a pirate ship was a mixed bag of crooks, scoundrels, thieves and escapees from different nationalities. Many were captured slaves or ex-slaves and language barriers were often a big problem.
The ship's Captain set the rules of conduct and assigned duties.
His word was law and his commands had to be followed to the letter. Anyone who disobeyed the Captain was severely punished by whipping, being thrown overboard or marooned on a deserted island. The crew usually slept in hammocks or in makeshift bedding laid out on the decks, provided the weather cooperated. Among the larger pirate ships, the Captain would recruit a navigator, sailmaker, ship's surgeon, blacksmith, carpenter and even a barrel maker. Repair of the ship was a constant job and at least once a year the ship

would be scuttled in shallow water to have its hull scraped of barnacles, oysters and seaworms that would infest the wooden planks. Daylight duties would involve repairing torn sails and ropes, scrubbing the decks, cleaning weapons of rust, greasing capstans and pulleys, killing rats, pumping out the bilges, and keeping a constant watch for potential enemy ships and new targets to attack. Sailing anywhere in the Caribbean meant keeping an eye out for dangerous reefs and other submerged objects. Winter months could bring cold weather and summer months surely brought unbearable heat and humidity. Mold was a constant problem and would contribute to the rotting of sails, food and clothing. Life was definitely rough onboard and many pirates lead double lives by having to support wives and children in far off countries. Health problems were a constant factor, especially scurvy brought on by a lack of vitamin C. The curative powers of eating citrus was not widely recognized until the 1800's.

After months or even weeks at sea, the pirates looked forward to visiting larger ports such as Port Royal, Jamaica where they could drink and gamble the nights away. Prostitution was rampant and so was the associated venereal diseases such as syphilis and gonorrhea. Many a pirate easily lost his share of ill gotten treasure in one or two nights, returning back to ship broke. Women generally would not be allowed on the pirate ships, however two famous women pirates (Mary Read and Anne Bonny) enlisted on pirate ships, dressed and acting as men. Later when their true identities were discovered, fellow pirates treated them with respect because of their fierce fighting capabilities. Anne Bonny eventually married "Calico Jack" Jack Rackham and then made a living as a married couple by raiding Spanish ships throughout the Caribbean basin.

LIFE ONBOARD
RULES OF CONDUCT

Pirates and sailors in the Caribbean were under strict Codes of Conduct. While the list of Conduct Rules varied somewhat according to the demands of different Captains, basic rules were always present. For example, Captain Bartholomew Roberts had his crew to swear to abide by the following:

1. Each crew member shall obey orders.

2. Booty will be shared as follows: 1 share for each ordinary seaman; 1-1/2 shares to the Captain; 1-1/4 shares to the ships master carpenter, boatswain and gunner.

3. Any member keeping a secret or planning a mutiny will be marooned. He can only take a flask of gunpowder, a bottle of water, a gun and some shot.

4. The punishment for hitting another crew member is 40 lashes.

5. Anyone not maintaining his gun properly will lose their share.

6. Everyone on the ship will have one vote when it comes to decisions on important matters.

7. Everyone shall have a share of captured food and drink, including fresh food.

8. Any crew member found stealing on the ship shall have his nose and ears split open and be set ashore.

9. Gambling with cards and money is forbidden on the ship.

10. The penalty of bringing a female on board in disguise is death.

11. Musicians onboard will have only one day a week off. (Note: Many Captains actually hired musicians to entertain the crew and to alarm and confuse the crew of any ship being attacked!)

12. No seaman may leave the rest of the crew until each man has made at least 1,000 British Pounds.

13. Any member losing a limb shall receive 800 silver dollars.

PIRATE FLAGS

The Pirate Flag originally was a red flag, perhaps a derivation from the French "Joli Rouge" (converted to the Jolly Roger by the English pirates). The English pirates began to use the black skull & crossbones, and later creating more individualized flags. Shown here are a few of the "special flags" used by specific pirates in conjunction with the standard Jolly Roger.

Thomas Tew

Blackbeard

Stede Bonnet

Jack Rackham

Christopher Moody

Captain Dulaien

Christopher Condent

PIRATE WEAPONS

1660-1730

Pirates used a variety of weapons which included pistols, blunderbuss, sabers, daggers, knives, cannons, and a variety of other weapons. Many weapons were often handmade by the pirates themselves.. one being a device that looked like an ice pick. Other weapons included whips and chains with a spiked-ball on the end. Flintlock rifles and muskets were used, usually for long range attacks and on land to hunt for game.

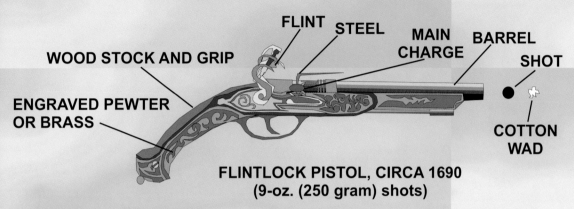

FLINT **STEEL** **MAIN CHARGE** **BARREL** **SHOT**

WOOD STOCK AND GRIP

ENGRAVED PEWTER OR BRASS

COTTON WAD

FLINTLOCK PISTOL, CIRCA 1690
(9-oz. (250 gram) shots)

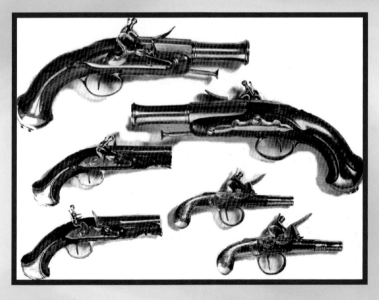

A COLLECTION OF PIRATE FLINTLOCK PISTOLS IN A PRIVATE COLLECTION, NASSAU, BAHAMAS

THE BETTER SWORDS, SABERS AND THE CUTLASS WERE USUALLY MADE IN SPAIN, PORTUGAL OR ENGLAND

PIRATE DAGGERS

PIRATE WEAPONS

1660-1730

The use of cannons by pirates were mainly for two purposes. 1. To threaten another vessel into stopping by shooting across their bow. Rarely did the pirates fire the cannons broadside into a ship being chased because of fear it may burn and sink before the booty was confiscated. Also the enemy ship itself may become a prize possession for the pirates. 2. The cannons, both small and large, were often used as a defensive weapon in the various forts that the pirates may have occupied.

A SALVAGED CANNONBALL AND GRAPESHOT RECOVERED FROM A PIRATE WRECK

A 17TH CENTURY DIAGRAM OF A CANNON

PIRATE DRESS

**BOTH MALE AND FEMALE PIRATES WORE A
LARGE VARIETY OF CLOTHING.. SOME VERY
ELEGANT AND OTHERS SIMPLY RAGS**

PIRATES FOOD AND DRINK

Dining on a pirate ship was at best boring! Only on a special occasion would the ship's cook prepare something even approaching a good meal. It was up to the ship's captain to set an allotment of food, especially when the journey in the Caribbean could last several weeks before shore-leave came.

The pirates menu was extremely varied and dependant upon locally available food sources. The captain of the ship usually chose the cheapest food available for the crew.. although at times he would have his own special stash of premium food, wine and/or rum. Cooking was accomplished by using a small charcoal stove on the deck. Sanitation was certainly lacking and fresh water was rarely used to wash the pots, pans, plates and utensils.

Because of lack of refrigeration, fresh meat, fruit and vegetables would last only a few days. Then on a long voyage, the menu would revert to what was called "barrel food". Barrel food consisted of salt pork, biscuits, bacon, peas and floor to make unleavened bread. Flies, maggots and rats always outnumbered the crew!

On bigger vessels, sailors or slaves who were often captured by pirates were in charge of running the ship. When not preparing food for the crew, the cook was responsible for catching fish to help supplement the menu.

During times of heavy battle, even sailors fought side by side with the pirates.

Here is a sample of a weeks allotment granted to each pirate and sailor.

One half pound of cheese
Three pounds of biscuits
One half pound of butter
One quart of vinegar
One pint of fresh water per day
On Sundays, three quarters pound of animal
flesh meat when available
Six ounces of salted cod every Tuesday and Thursday
One pound of boiled grey peas
Three quarters of a pound of bacon
As much oatmeal that could be eaten for breakfast
One pint or grog of rum per day during the evening

**FRESH FRUIT WAS USUALLY A LUXURY
EXCEPT WHEN IN PORT AT THE LARGER
CARIBBEAN ISLANDS**

PIRATE TREASURE & ARTIFACTS

A "BLOCK" OF SILVER PIECES-OF-EIGHT RECOVERED FROM A PIRATE WRECK. THE WOODEN CHEST HAD ROTTED AWAY AFTER SOME 250 YEARS OF LAYING ON THE OCEAN FLOOR.

A PIRATE'S PEWTER MUG AND GLASS RUM BOTTLE RECOVERED FROM THE CARIBBEAN

PIRATE'S SPOON AND A PESTLE FOR GRINDING MEDICINE

PIRATE TREASURE COINS

Gold Doubloons

The gold doubloon was a favorite among the pirates. Minted in the new Spanish Colonies of the Americas, gold doubloons were made as 8, 4, 2 and 1 Escudos. Pictured here is the 4 Escudo doubloon which contains 13.7340 grams of gold.

OBVERSE

- Spanish Crown
- Minted in Lima, Peru
- Pillars of Hercules
- Year: 1692
- Legend: "And of the Indies..King"
- 4 Escudo
- Assayer "M"
- Plus Ultra
- Ocean waves (signifying the new Spanish Empire)

Shown Enlarged
Today's Value: About $2,200.

REVERSE

- Castillo (Castle)
- Jerusalem Cross
- Legend: "Carlos II...And of the Spains"
- Leon (Lion)
- Note the irregular edges of these Doubloons

THE PILLAR DOLLAR

So-called because it includes the "Pillars of Hercules" in the design. This Spanish "8 Reales" silver coin replaced the older "Pieces-of-Eight" silver coins which were also called "Cobs". Minting of this basic design began in 1732 and continued for less than 100 years. The coin above was minted in Mexico City. Note the letter "M" with the small "o" over it. This coin is sometimes referred to as the "Post-Piracy" coin, although many a pirate "collected" these coins.

10 or 12 of these coins in good condition will buy you a new Rolls Royce!

Very valuable gold 8 Escudo gold Spanish coins minted in Bogota, Colombia in 1765. Note the "clipped edges" which indicate the mint had removed enough gold to make sure each coin weighed the required 22-28 grams.

PIRATE TREASURE COINS

Pieces-of-Eight

Only silver coins were called Pieces-of-Eight. They were also called the English name COB. Silver coins of the Spanish Colonies were made in 8, 4, 2, 1 and 1/2 Reales. The weight of a 8 Escudo or 8 Reale was 27.4680 grams. Pirates usually buried more silver coins than gold coins...even though their relative value was quite different.

OBVERSE

Spanish Crown

Monarch's Shield
Felipe III

Minted in Potisi, Bolivia

8 Reales

Assayer: Unknown

Legend:
"And of the Indies..King"

Shown Reduced
Today's Value: About $1,200.

REVERSE

Year: 1619

Leon
(Lion)

Castillo
(Castle)

Cross

Legend:
Felipe III...And of the Spains"

Note the irregular edges.
These silver coins were
also known as "COBS".

An old engraving depicting Pirates and Buccaneers in the Caribbean trading and dividing treasure coins, silver plates and other precious artifacts among crew members.

PIRATE TREASURE

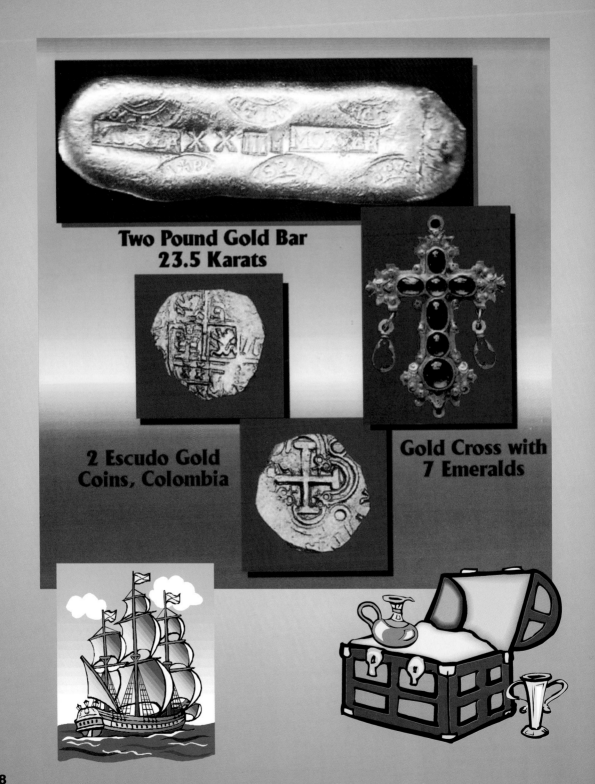

Two Pound Gold Bar
23.5 Karats

2 Escudo Gold
Coins, Colombia

Gold Cross with
7 Emeralds

PIRATE DOCUMENTS

Very few original documents pertaining to piracy have survived. Below are three documents: A real pirate treasure map that was drawn upon the recollections of a retired pirate; a broadside advertising the trial of pirate Jack Rackham; and a sketch of ocean creatures that superstitious pirates believed existed.

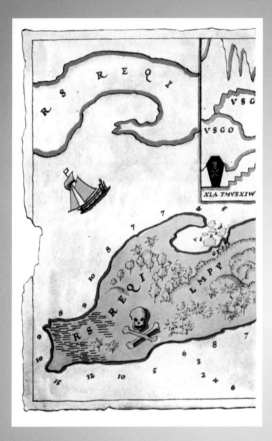

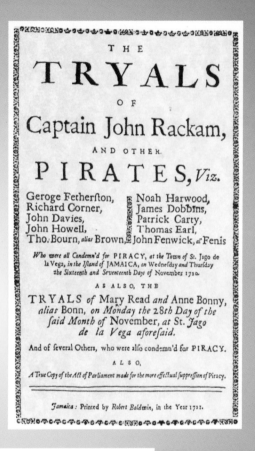

PIRATES ONSHORE

Many Caribbean pirates opted to sail the seas only a few months of the year. Meanwhile, other pirates retired and built little homes on many Caribbean islands. Most of the pirates changed their identities and remained silent about their life of piracy. Some pirates even built a church in St. Thomas which later burned down! From the Bahamas to Barbados.. descendants of these pirates can still be found living on the islands of the Caribbean. Without doubt, life on land was much easier.

A typical Pirate house dating back 220 years (with some modern renovations). The houses were usually one room, with shuttered windows and located near the shore for cool breezes. This house is still in use, and can be found on Tortola, British Virgin Islands..a favorite haunt of pirate acitivity. Note the 2 front doors!

Many pirates raised animals, and grew fruits and vegetables, Favorite animals were goats, chickens and pigs, Some pirates learned how to smoke meat from the French Boucaniers of Hispanola...often trading the meat to passing ships for rum, tea, tobacco, clothing and shoes. A typical Caribbean pirate garden could contain yams, manioc, maize, garlic, squash, mangos, guava, breadfruit, bananas, papayas, limes, oranges, coconuts. The nearby sea provided fresh fish, lobsters, crabs and turtles. Other wild delicacies included pigeons and iguanas! Cooking was usually done outside on a charcoal or wood burning stove. A separate smokehouse was common.

FAMOUS CARIBBEAN PIRATES

Edward Teach

Blackbeard was one of the most famous and notorious pirates of the Caribbean! Born Edward Drummond in Bristol, England in the late 1600's, he went to sea as a youth on a merchant ship. In 1716, he changed his name to Edward Teach. Later as his hair and large, jet black beard began to grow, Edward would take on the name of Blackbeard. By this time he had successfully captured many ships and looted them for their cargoes. He would place "homemade" firecrackers in his beard and hair...lighting them during a battle. This demonic look of his hair smoking and exploding gave him an obvious fearsome look. His favorite hangout was Charlotte Amalie, St. Thomas, although he would take several extended cruises off the coast of North Carolina. The island of Ocracoke was another hangout and it was here he would repair his ship. In 1718, he captured 8 or 9 gold laden ships in Charleston Harbor including taking several local citizens into captivity..holding them for ransom until medicine for his crew arrived. Blackbeard married at least 14 wives and most he never bothered to divorce! His final battle was fought against a Lt. Robert Maynard of the Royal Navy while attacking Maynard's sloop. Countless cutlass wounds and five pistol shots finally ended Blackbeard's notorious career on November 17, 1718.

Captain Henry Morgan

Henry Morgan, born in 1635 to a Welsh farmer, sailed to Barbados as an indentured servant. From Barbados, Morgan sailed to Tortuga and joined "The Brethren of the Coast"..becoming a formidable pirate. One of his first raids was on southern Cuba, where his men went from house to house, village to village on a murderous rampage. It was here he slaughtered 500 oxen and salted the meat for the crews of his ships. From Cuba he raided Porto Bello, Panama. Soon to follow were other ports along the South American coast and then northward to Jamaica. In Jamaica he found a second life, took a wife and then began acquiring property. His new career as a land owner was abruptly ended when he was asked to attack Panama. Morgan sailed with 36 ships filled with experienced pirates and buccaneers and conquered Panama in few days! Returning to Jamaica with untold wealth, Morgan was greeted as a hero. His life then turned to politics for some years and he was knighted as lieutenant-governor of Jamaica. His wealth was responsible for Port Royal's growth. There was one tavern for every nine residents in Port Royal! In 1668, Sir Henry Morgan died. Then four years later, a devastating earthquake sank Port Royal and Morgans grave ended into the depths of the sea!

FAMOUS CARIBBEAN PIRATES

BARTHOLOMEW ROBERTS

Bartholomew Roberts was born in 1682 in Wales. Roberts probably became a pirate at the age of 37 years. He holds a "pirate record" of sorts...being the only pirate known that captured over 400 ships in less than 3 years! This averaged over 2 ships per week! After a successful raid on a fleet of Portuguese ships setting sail from Brasil, Roberts sailed north to party. Stopping off at Devils Island, French Guiana, he found a royal welcome... even from the governor. Hated by the governors of Barbados and Martinique, Roberts designed his own personal pirate flag as an act of defiance. Of the many ports of call he made, Roberts would always reserve a last minute decision as to whether just visit the port or to ransack it! In the early 1700's, the manufacturing of rum was popular in the West Indies and many ships carried hundreds of barrels of this valuable cargo. More than one rum cargo ship was captured and at least one rum warehouse was emptied of it's contents and then burned to the ground. Surprisingly, Roberts was not a drinker and wanted to discourage the drinking of spirits on his ships. He realized this was not realistic because of the characters of his crew. Therefore the best he could do was to enforce the rules of the ship which allowed rum drinking only at certain hours of the day. In February 1722, Roberts met his end in a battle while at anchor off the Cape in South Africa.

Gustav Wilmerding

Gustav Wilmerding was the pirate emperor of Tortola, British Virgin Islands. On his first sailing from Denmark as a twelve year old cabin boy, he was captured by a pirate ship in the Caribbean. Intrigued by his captors, Wilmerding decided to also become a pirate. Although little is know about this secretive pirate, Wilmerding eventually had his own ship and operated from Sopers Hole on the west end of the island of Tortola. Sopers Hole was chosen for it's protected deep water harbor, and the surrounding hills afforded excellent locations for batteries of cannons. Less than 20 miles from St. Thomas, this location proved to be a safer landbase for pirate activities than did the wicked and larger pirate settlement of Charlotte Amalie.

Wilmerding was famous for having a band of musicians onboard his pirate ship. Songs, especially beating rhythms from drums, bewildered his enemies into easy surrender. This musical pirate earned the nickname of "Ding Ding". After 40 years of successful piracy in the Caribbean, Wilmerding decided to take his ill-gotten wealth and retire to Little Thatch island just west of Sopers Hole. Here he constructed his home and also housing for several young maidens. His wealth allowed him to dress the girls in the finest silks and he showered them with gifts of gold and silver jewelry. Remnants of his house can still be seen.

FAMOUS CARIBBEAN PIRATES

Pierre le Grand

Pierre le Grand, alias One-Eyed Jack, was a French pirate. Losing his eye in a questionable sea battle, le Grand became one of the most cruelest pirates in the Caribbean. Little is known of him, other than his fame to glory was that he became the first pirate captain to capture a full laden treasure galleon sailing to Spain. He is also considered the father of buccaneers, having lived on the land in Hispaniola for several years. Here he hunted wild cattle and pigs in the hills, smoked the meat, raised some tobacco and traded with other pirates stopping on the south coast of Hispaniola for provisions. After realizing the amount of money the pirates had to spend at his meager provisions store, le Grand finally decided to take to the sea. He actually paid for his first pirate ship and had it outfitted with cannons and other armaments. Taking over a year to finish his ship, le Grand finally set sail with a raggedy crew of about 30 men. Speed of his ship was important to him and at least twice a year, le Grand would career his ship at low tide to remove the barnacles and to make repairs. A lover of women, he would allow his men and himself the luxury of staying in port for a month or more...indulging in wine, women and song. Pirate le Grand preferred to attack during a moonlit night while the unsuspecting quarry lay at anchor. No one is certain how or when he finally died...rumor being he retired in Martinique or in St. Martin.

Mary Read

Mary Read was one of the most infamous female pirates of the Caribbean. While some historians believe that as many as 100 or more female pirates existed at one time or another, only a few stand out. Mary Read was one of them. As a young woman, Mary was attractive. In her later years her personal appearance drastically changed. The harsh life on board a pirate ship had taken it's toll on her looks and behavior! Mary was actually thought of being a young seaman when she was captured along with her shipmates by Calico Jack. Mary Read was born in Ireland and became a runaway, hiding as a man for several years. At one time, Mary even joined the British Army and later the British Navy. She served as a seaman, totally unnoticed as to her real gender. Later she married and began to dress as a woman. However after her husband died, Mary sold the family tavern and converted back to a "male" seaman, joining a Dutch ship. When the Dutch ship was captured by Calico Jack, Mary revealed her true gender and signed the pirate articles. For years she was one of the best pirates because of her agility. Later a romance began between her and Calico Jack. Eventually she and Calico Jack stood trial for piracy. While Calico Jack received a sentence of hanging, Mary escaped the same fate because of her pregnancy. She is believed to have died of a fever in a prison in her later years.

FAMOUS CARIBBEAN PIRATES

**BLUEBEARD'S WATCHTOWER
IN ST. THOMAS, U.S.V.I.**

**BLUEBEARD RAISING
THE JOLLY ROGER**

SOME OTHER PIRATES OF THE CARIBBEAN ISLANDS

A Frenchman born Giles de Rais became the infamous pirate Bluebeard. In 1689 Bluebeard picked a prime location in the hills above Charlotte Amalie, St. Thomas and constructed a round watchtower of local rock. From here he could see in all directions to keep watch for ships entering and leaving the harbor at Charlotte Amalie.

Sam Bellamy in the early 1700s (also known as Black Sam) left his native Devon, England to join a privateering force then at war against the Spaniards. After the end of the war in 1723, Black Sam decided to command a pirate crew. Under his command, Black Sam captured and looted some fifty ships between Tortola and St. Thomas. Worried that the British Navy knew of his hideout, Black Sam finally set sail in his newly acquired ship Whidah. On the night of April 26th, a fierce storm came upon them and the entire crew including Black Sam drowned.

CARIBBEAN RUM HISTORY

From the sun drenched islands of the Florida Keys, The Bahamas, Cuba, Puerto Rico, Hispaniola, The Virgin Islands, Jamaica, Cayman Islands and down to Barbados and Trinidad, rum has become the king of alcoholic drinks since being created some 400 years ago.

Perhaps no other drink in the world has had such a history tied to it. And it all began in 1492 when Columbus decided to explore, conquer and occupy the Caribbean Basin.

Still called the West Indies today, Columbus thought he had found a new route to India. Caribbean island settlements began to be established by the Portuguese, Spanish, Dutch, Danish, French and English. Competition to claim the various islands was fierce and lasted for several hundred years. The Europeans soon realized that the islands offered an excellent place to establish large plantations to cultivate a newly imported plant from the Far East known as sugar cane. Soon Europe and the newly settled colonies of the United States began to place demands on importing tropical products such as cotton. This was the first cash crop of the Caribbean and it was soon followed by the sweet product known as sugar.. including molasses and rum.

The warm Caribbean islands had perfect weather but first the land had to be cleared for cultivation. It took years to clear all the land that was necessary to cultivate, harvest and process sugar cane to meet the demand.

Although the Spanish and Portuguese had perfected rum making years before in Brasil, their attempt to keep these processes secret for the islands failed.

When the Dutch settlers began sugar cane production in the Caribbean, they excelled in engineering achievements such as designing and constructing the wind driven sugar mills. Soon, they became the island masters at creating superb rum.

For the next three centuries, the Caribbean islands produced a multitude of different flavored rums and that same tradition continues today.

While rum was being made in the islands, the new U. S. Colonies preferred to import mostly the raw molasses and do the distilling in their own facilities. Thus began active trade between the U. S. and the various Caribbean islands.

What is left to see today of these original sugar cane plantations? A visit to most any island of substantial size will reveal relics of many old plantations, their Great Houses, the cleared plots of land once green with sugar cane, the wind driven sugar mills used to crush the cane and remnants of old rum factories. A few islands still produce rum in these original stone constructed rum distilleries, relying on the same water driven technology installed hundreds of years ago.

EARLY CARIBBEAN RUM

GROWING AND CUTTING SUGAR CANE WAS THE FIRST STEP IN MAKING RUM.

SOME CARIBBEAN ISLANDS HAD 150 SUGAR MILLS OPERATING AT ONE TIME.

BURROS, MULES, DONKEYS AND OXEN WERE IMPORTED TO THE ISLANDS TO HAUL THE CANE TO THE SUGAR MILLS.

U. S. Virgin Islands

The History of Rum Making · Harvesting Sugar Cane

Caribbean rum had its island roots thanks to Christopher Columbus. Sugar cane was brought to Puerto Rico from the Orient in 1502. Land was cleared and planting of sugar cane began. Soon after, sugar plantations spread rapidly to other islands. Some 18 months after planting, the sugar cane was harvested and brought to the sugar mills where wind driven crushers squeezed the juice out of the cane.

THE SUGAR MILLS WERE CONSTRUCTED OF STONE, CORAL ROCK AND EVEN SEASHELLS.

THIS WOODEN POST MOVED THE TOP "GEAR HOUSE" STRUCTURE ON THE SUGAR MILL TO FACE THE WIND FOR MAXIMUM SPEED OF THE CRUSHING ROLLERS.

INSIDE THE SUGAR MILL WERE THE CRUSHING ROLLERS.

THE SUGAR MILL WAS USUALLY PLACED ON A HIGH HILL TO CATCH THE WIND. THE SUGAR CANE JUICE FLOWED DOWNHILL IN WOODEN RACEWAYS TO THE BOILING HOUSE.

THE BLADES OF THE SUGAR MILL POINTED IN THE DIRECTION WHERE THE WIND WAS THE STRONGEST.

PUERTO RICO

The History of Rum Making · Grinding Sugar Cane

Holland developed the wind driven sugar mills that dotted the islands. Sugar cane was harvested and crushed at the sugar mill between wind driven crushing rollers. On windless days, sugar cane was crushed at another site by animal powered crushers. The juice extracted from the cane flowed downhill to storage vats at the distillery.

EARLY CARIBBEAN RUM

THE COPPER POT STILL WAS A FAVORITE IN RUM MAKING.

THE BIG WOODEN VAT CONTAINED COLD WATER. THE CONDENSER COIL CONDENSES THE HOT VAPORS INTO RUM LIQUOR WHEN COOLED BY THE VAT WATER. RUM POURS OUT AT THE BOTTOM FAUCET.

HOT VAPORS CONTAINING ALCOHOL AND RUM VAPORS ENTER THE CONDENSING COILS.

RUM IS POURED FROM COLLECTING PAILS INTO STORAGE BARRELS, READY FOR AGING AND SHIPPING.

JAMAICA

The History of Rum Making • Rum Distillery

White rum was made from straight sugar cane juice by using yeast to ferment it into alcohol. Later molasses, which was a byproduct of making sugar, became the prime ingredient in rum making. Molasses combined with yeast, water and citrus flavorings produced fermentation which changed the sugar molecules into a low grade rum alcohol. The alcohol was then condensed in stills of different configurations, resulting in a fairly clear rum, full of flavor and with increased alcohol content. The clear rum was then placed into charred oak barrels and allowed to age in storage barns. The oak barrel (still used today) added traditional rum flavor and color. The longer the rum remained in the oak barrels, a darker and richer rum developed.

BARRELS OF RUM WERE ROLLED INTO WAITING SKIFFS, THEN LIFTED WITH ROPE AND TACKLE INTO THE SHIPS HOLE.

LATER, AS EXPORTS GREW, DOCKS WERE BUILT TO ACCOMMODATE LARGE VESSELS THAT CARRIED THE RUM TO EUROPE AND THE U. S. COLONIES.

BARBADOS

The History of Rum Making • Transportation

Rum was shipped to waiting boats in large wooden barrels. Sugar was usually shipped in smaller kegs called "hogsheads" because of its weight.

TYPES OF CARIBBEAN RUM

It is generally accepted that there are 8 categories that most rum can be placed into. Price does not necessarily indicate the quality of rum. Often an inexpensive rum works the best in mixed drinks. The best way to find out is to simply experiment with a variety of rums and you will find what works for you!

White, Light
Clear colored rum generally unaged.

Gold, Golden
Medium bodied rum, slightly sweet, aged in oak barrels. Stronger flavor in mixed drinks.

Dark, Black
Medium to long aging in very charred oak barrels. Perfect for sipping, full bodied and aromatic.

Premium, Anejo
This rum is amber hued in color and many considered it to be the "cognac" of rums. Best when sipped from a brandy glass.

Single Marks
Very premium aged rum, not blended. Since the rum comes from different oak barrels, bottles may vary in flavor. Usually produced in very limited quantities at a premium price. Definitely a sipping rum.

Overproof
As it's names implies, higher concentrate of alcohol is added to the rum. 151 Proof rum is an example of this type of rum.

Flavored
Base rum where flavors such as coconut, orange, banana or pineapple are added. Very popular in the Caribbean.

Spiced
The flavor of spiced rum varies from island to island and distillery to distillery. As many as 15 different spices can be blended to create a spiced rum. Many spice formulas are kept secret by the distillery.

RUM PRODUCTION IN THE CARIBBEAN ISLANDS

TOP RUM PRODUCING ISLANDS
Trinidad
Barbados
Puerto Rico
Cuba
Jamaica
Martinique
Guadeloupe
U. S. Virgin Islands

(CUBA)

HAITI DOMINICAN REPUBLIC

PUERTO RICO

TORTOLA B.V.I.
ST. JOHN
ST. THOMAS
U.S.V.I.
ST. CROIX
ST. MARTIN/
ST. MAARTEN
ST. BARTS
BARBUDA
ST. EUSTATIUS
ST. KITTS
ANTIGUA
NEVIS

JAMAICA

Caribbean Sea

GUADELOUPE
MARIA-GALANTE
DOMINICA

Atlantic Ocean

MARTINIQUE

ST. LUCIA

ST. VINCENT

BARBADOS

GRENADINES

TRINIDAD

GRENADA

RUM NOTES...

British sailors on duty in the West Indies (Caribbean) in 1731 were given a daily ration of ½ pint rum. Rationing of rum was changed in 1740 by Admiral Edward Vernon (nick-named "Old Grogram"). The name was shortened by his sailors to "grog".. as the name for the new ration. Later.. pirates adopted the same custom, but they acquired rum mostly from their own acts of piracy.

POPULAR GLASSES FOR SERVING RUM

Highball, Tall

Collins

Old Fashioned/Rocks

Champagne Daiquiri Margarita

Rumrunner

Tropical

Fancy Cruise Ship

Brandy Sniffer

Champagne Flute

PIRATES AND RUM

PIRATES WHO LOVED RUM

Blackbeard (Captain Teach)
Henry Morgan
Calico Jack (Captain Jack Rackham)
Captain Richard Sawkins
Captain Bartholomew Roberts

The French spelling
for rum is..
RHUM

Pirates and rum have always been synonymous in Caribbean history. Although pirates preferred to steal barreled rum because of its bulk value.. bottled rum was also sought after. Bottles of hand blown glass or ceramic were originally made in Europe and shipped empty to the Caribbean. At the distillery they were filled with mostly premium aged rum.. then placed into wood crates and sent to European destinations.

Later, hand blown glass and ceramic bottles of various shapes were made on several Caribbean islands.

Today, divers occasionally still find barnacle covered "pirate" rum bottles dating back to the 17th, 18th and 19th centuries. Port Royal, Jamaica was a "pirate capitol" for years until destroyed in an earthquake. Many rum bottles have been discovered there.

PIRATE RUM DRINKS

PIRATES'S PLEASURE

1 1/2 oz Golden Rum
1/2 oz Sweet Vermouth
1/2 oz fresh Lemon Juice
1/2 oz fresh Orange Juice
1/4 oz Sugar Syrup
2 dashes Angostura Bitters
Nutmeg
Cinnamon

Shake with cracked ice and strain
into cocktail glass. Sprinkle nutmeg
and cinnamon on top. Serves 1.

PIRATE'S DARK HOLE

2 1/2 oz Dark Rum
1 tsp Spiced Rum
1 tsp Brown Sugar
1/4 tsp fresh Lime Juice
chilled Soda Water

Place ice cubes into a tall old
fashioned glass. Add dark rum. Stir
in brown sugar. Add soda water.
Squeeze lime juice wedge on top.
Stir once more. Serves 1.

BLUEBEARD'S WENCH

1 1/2 oz Light Rum
1/2 oz Lemon Juice
1/2 oz Blue Curacao
1/2 oz Cointreau

Shake with ice and strain into a
cocktail glass. Decorate with a
cherry. Serves 1.

PIRATE RUM DRINKS

PIRATE RUM SWIZZLE

juice of 1 Lime
1 tsp Powdered Sugar
2 oz Club Soda
2 dash Bitters
2 oz Light or Dark Rum

Put lime juice, sugar, and 2 oz club soda into collins glass. Fill glass with ice and stir. Add bitters and rum. Fill with club soda and serve with a swizzle stick. Serves 1.

PIRATE'S PATCH

1 1/4 oz 151-proof White Rum
3/4 oz Melon Liqueur
4 oz Orange Juice

Shake and pour into hurricane or parfait glass filled with ice. Serves 1.

PIRATE LIME RICKY

juice of 1/2 Key Lime
1 1/2 oz Light Rum
cold Club Soda

Pour into highball glass over ice cubes and fill with club soda and ice cubes. Stir. Add a wedge of lime. Serves 1.

PIRATE'S PASSION

3/4 oz Premium Dark Rum
1/2 oz Kiwi Schnapps
1/2 oz Strawberry Schnapps
3/4 glass of cold Lemon/Lime soda
Ice

Mix rum, kiwi and strawberry schnapps into a shaker with ice. Fill a glass 3/4 full of cold lemon/lime soda. Serves 1.

PIRATE SUNSET

3/4 oz Light Rum
3/4 oz Brandy
juice of 1/4 Lemon
2 tsp Raspberry Syrup

Shake with ice and strain into cocktail glass. Add fruit slices to rim. If available.. float fresh raspberries on top. Serves 1.